VIKING
ADVENTURE
Activity Book

Illustrated by Jen Alliston

Button
BOOKS

The Vikings lived in northern Europe just over a thousand years ago. These sailors, traders, and warriors, also known as Norse people, set sail to explore new lands. Fierce and clever, they were feared wherever they went, but they were also skilled at making things and telling stories. So let's set sail and have some Viking fun!

The world of the Vikings

Vikings came from Norway, Sweden, and Denmark, and about 1,200 years ago they went exploring. They set sail in their longships to find places to raid and sometimes settle in. Follow the paths of the ships to see where these Norse invaders went. Then use the stickers in the middle of the book to label those countries.

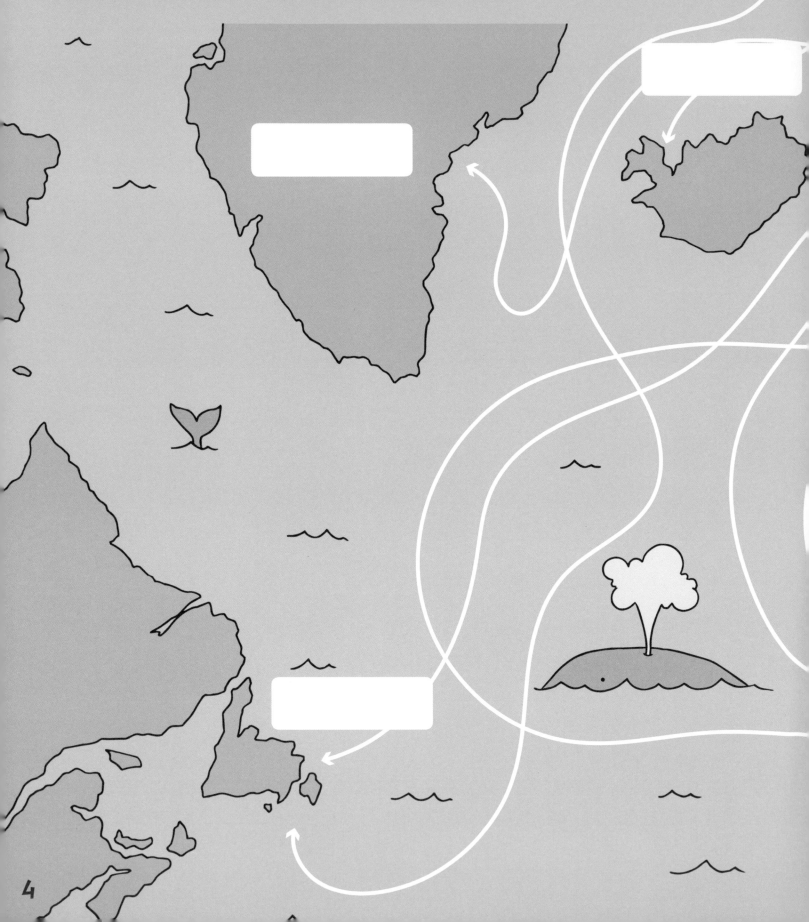

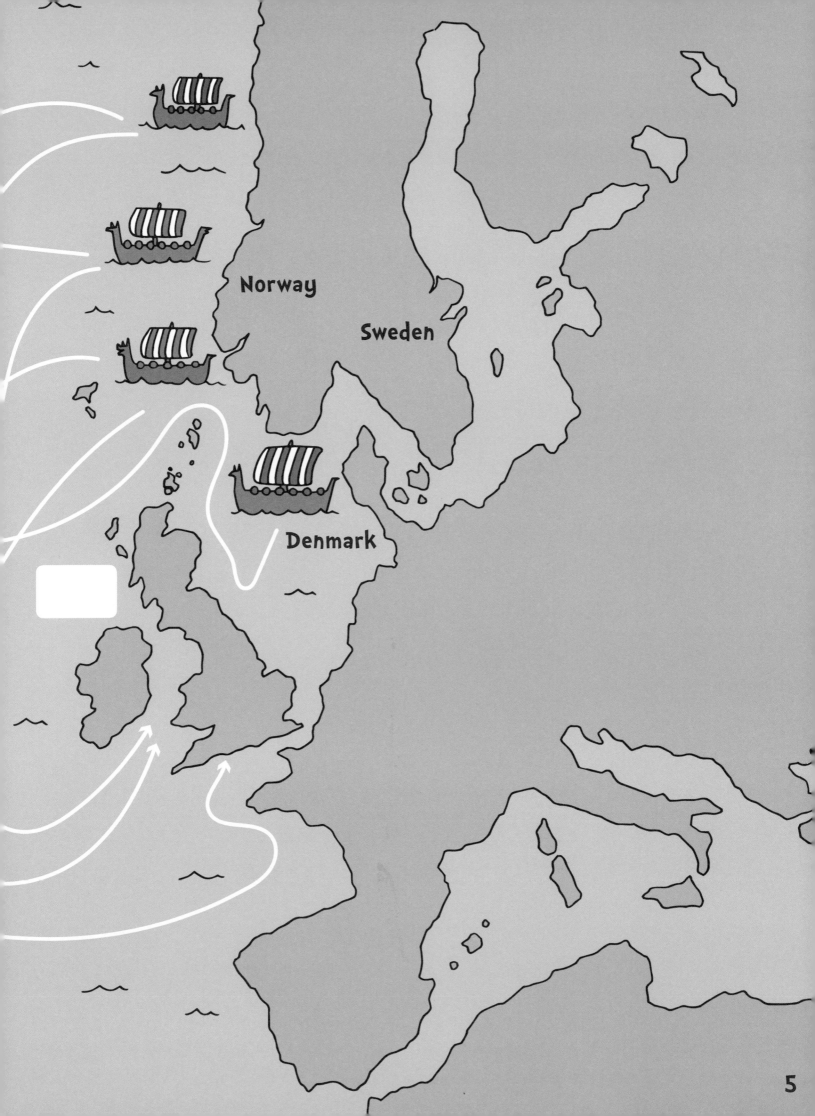

Norway

Sweden

Denmark

Meet the Viking warrior

Can you use the descriptions to number the different parts of this Viking's outfit?

❶ Shield

Vikings used round shields made of wood to protect them during battle.

❷ Chain-mail tunic

Warriors wore these heavy tunics to protect them in battle.

❸ Helmet

We think of Vikings wearing horned helmets, but there is no proof that they did. Instead they favored headgear with nose guards or visors to protect the face.

❹ Cloak

Viking cloaks were made from wool or animal skins and were arranged so the warrior's fighting arm was free.

❺ Brooch

Vikings loved jewelry and they used brooches instead of buttons or zips to fasten their clothing.

❻ Leather shoes

To protect their feet they wore shoes, often made of goatskin.

❼ Sword

Viking swords were double-edged and often decorated with copper or silver.

Odd figurehead out

Vikings liked to frighten their enemies with scary carvings called figureheads on the front of their ships. Can you spot the odd one out? Then color them all in.

Tall order

Viking women had a lot of power for the time. They could divorce their husbands and get involved in politics. Can you put these women in order of height? Number them from 1 for the smallest to 5 for the tallest.

Dotty boat building

Vikings were skilled sailors. Their longships were powered by sail out at sea or could be rowed in shallower waters or when there was no wind. Join the dots to complete this longship.

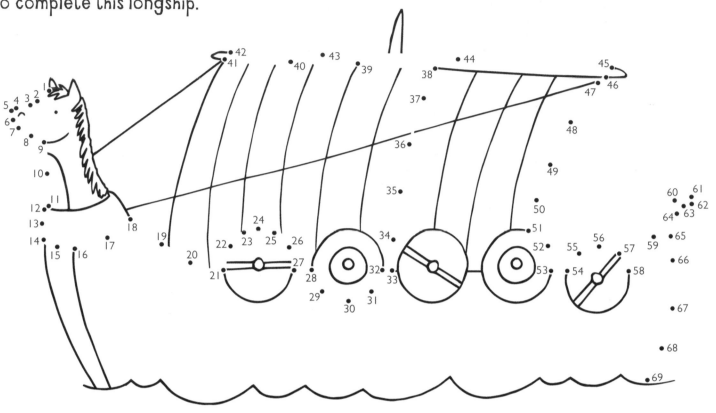

Get packing

Harald the Forgetful is off on a raid. Check the list to see what he has left behind by mistake.

Sword

Helmet

Shield

Brooch

Comb

Cloak

Oar

Ax

Drinking horn

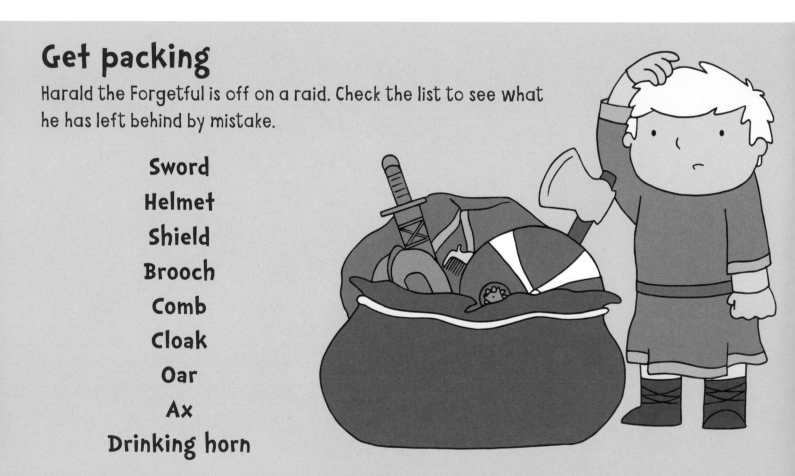

Norse jobs

As well as being ferocious warriors, Vikings were good at lots of other things.
Can you unscramble the letters to work out what these people did?

BOATBUILDER
JEWELER
FARMER
BASKETMAKER

RSKBEMATEKA

_ _ _ _ _ _ _ _ _ _ _

MEFRAR

_ _ _ _ _ _

OATUIBDERLB

_ _ _ _ _ _ _ _ _ _ _

WLEJEER

_ _ _ _ _ _ _

Raven guide

On long journeys Vikings would take a raven with them and set it free when they were out of sight of land. They'd watch which way it flew and if it didn't come back they knew that land was near. Can you help Erik the raven find his way to land through the maze?

Norse myths

Viking stories were full of the adventures of the gods. Can you match the names of these characters to the pictures?

_ _ _ _ _   _ _ _ _ _   _ _ _ _ _

Bragi
Bragi was the god of music and poetry. He was very good at playing the harp.

Thor
The god of thunder, Thor was strong and powerful, and famous for hitting monsters and mountains with his hammer.

Frigg
Goddess of the sky, Frigg would sit at her spinning wheel, making clouds. She also had magical powers that meant she could change the future.

- - - - -   - - - - -   - - - - -

Baldr
The son of Odin and Frigg, he was said to be so bright that light shone out of him.

Odin
The father of the gods, Odin had two raven friends called Huginn and Muninn. They flew around the world and brought back information for him.

Loki
A god of fire, Loki was known as a trickster who was able to change his appearance.

Odd brooch out

Viking men and women loved jewelry, especially brooches, which they used to fasten their clothing. Can you work out which of these brooches is the odd one out?

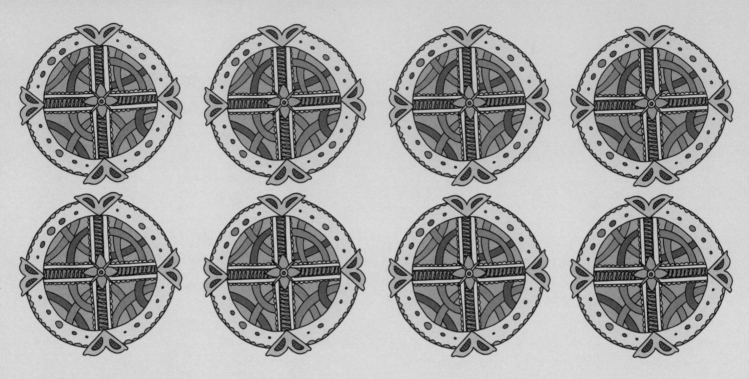

Norse wordsearch

There are lots of Viking words still used in English. Can you find these in the grid?

KNIFE

GLITTER

RANSACK

ANGER

EGG

CAKE

GLOVE

FOG

```
D R S V B R T Q G P N M C F T V C
L N G X R F N W D G Y J K N I F E
R S B Y T T D M B N S P C K R O C
D Q R P G M R S P R R Q S E G G K
Y B G L I T T E R K X N H P K H
F N W E F D H K A G W L Z S T R P
C G J S D K J H N L P V W P S B C
V L R X T R D G S R F R D K Y D A
Q O D Y U C S E A N G E R D P N K
X V L P T P Z B C K M D S K J R E
J E K F S V C L K N C A K T D T P
I W R B N R K J Y P B N S D M N K
```

Wardrobe raid

These Vikings are getting ready for a journey. Use the stickers to dress them up.

Longship races

These longships are having a race. Do the math problem to see which wins. The ship with the highest number is the fastest.

$$4 - 3 + 9 =$$

$$8 - 3 + 9 =$$

$$9 + 5 - 7 =$$

Make a Viking helmet

Real Vikings didn't have horns on their helmets (this was something made up in the 19th century), but they sometimes had wings. They also featured nose guards and visors to protect the face. You can make a helmet with all these things or just some of them.

Ask a grown-up to help!

You'll need:

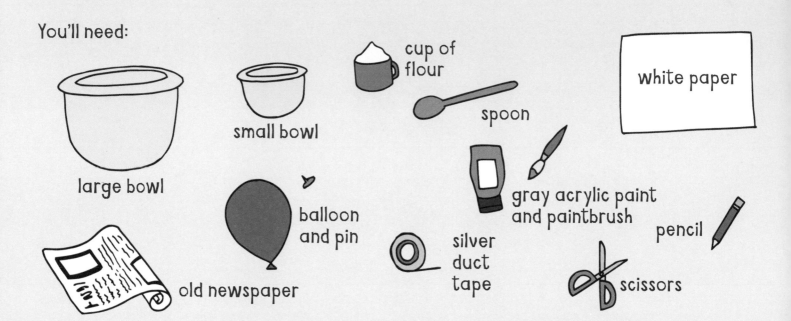

large bowl

small bowl

cup of flour

spoon

white paper

balloon and pin

gray acrylic paint and paintbrush

pencil

old newspaper

silver duct tape

scissors

 1. In a large bowl, mix a cup of flour with two cups of water to make a smooth paste.

 2. Rip the newspaper into small pieces and put in the bowl.

 3. Blow up the balloon so it is about the same size as your head and place it on a small bowl.

4. Put the sticky newspaper on the balloon until the top half is covered. Leave to dry for a few hours. Add a second layer and allow that to dry too. Continue until you have added up to five layers.

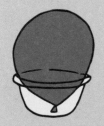 5. Next day, once the helmet is completely dry, burst the balloon with a pin and remove. Try the helmet on to work out where to trim so the helmet sits just above your eyebrows. Cut a neat edge with scissors.

 6. Paint the surface with gray acrylic paint and leave to dry. You may need a second coat.

7. Once it's dry, stick silver duct tape around the bottom edge of your helmet, tucking it underneath.

8. To make a visor, copy the template onto a piece of paper. Paint it gray and then cut it out with scissors. Make sure you cut out the eye holes too! Stick the visor to the front of your helmet using silver duct tape.

9. Stick strips of silver duct tape over the top of the helmet, from back to front, and side to side. If you want to make a nose guard, leave an end of tape at the front twice as long as your nose. Fold it in half and stick it to itself so that it will hang down in front of your nose.

10. For the wings, copy the template twice onto a folded piece of paper, making sure the flat edge is against the fold. Cut out and draw feather details on both sides in pencil, using the template as a guide. Cut the tab area in half along the fold.

11. Cut two slits in the sides of the helmet and slot in the tabs of the wings. Open the tabs out and use duct tape to fix them to the inside of the helmet.

12. Now proudly wear your helmet!

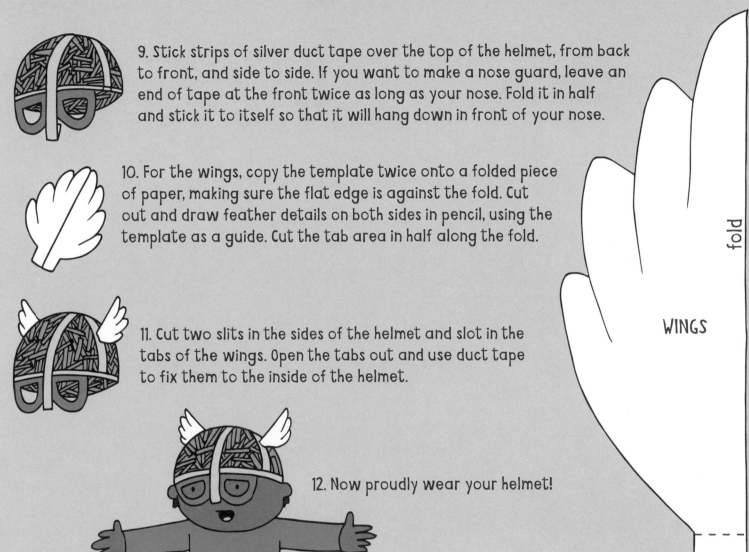

WINGS

fold

tab

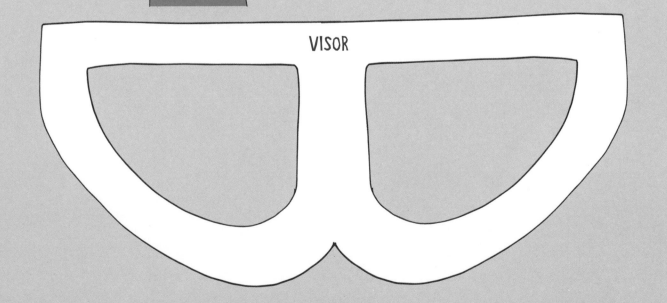

VISOR

Sky rider

Odin, the wise father of the Norse gods, had a magical horse with eight legs that could gallop through the air. Color in this picture of Odin and his horse Sleipnir.

How many stars can you count in the picture?

Eastern promise

As well as exploring to the west and north, Vikings also traveled east. They sailed along rivers as far as what is now Turkey to trade, selling wool, wheat, and leather and buying silk, silver, and spices. Find the stickers that match the items that they traded.

Treasure hunt

One of the first Viking raids on England was at the island of Lindisfarne in 793CE.
The monks who lived there had no weapons but lots of treasures. Can you spot where
these monks have tried to hide their five golden crosses from the Vikings?

Norse code

Vikings used an alphabet called runes to cut messages into stones and wood. The letters were made of straight lines so they were easy to carve.

These are the symbols the Vikings used and the letters they represent.

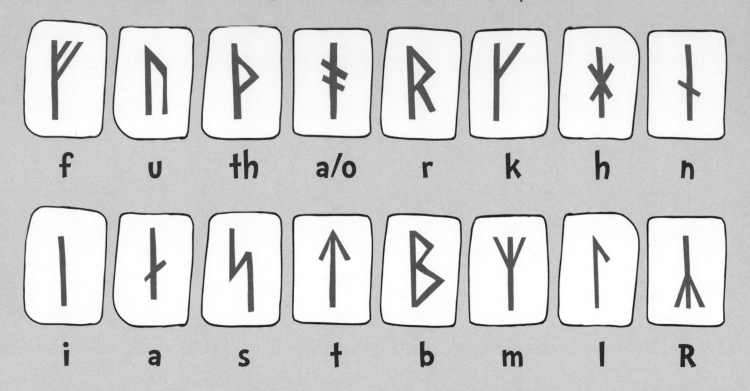

f   u   th   a/o   r   k   h   n

i   a   s   t   b   m   l   R

This is Ulf's special comb, which you can read about on the next page. Color it in and see if you can write Ulf's name on it in runes.

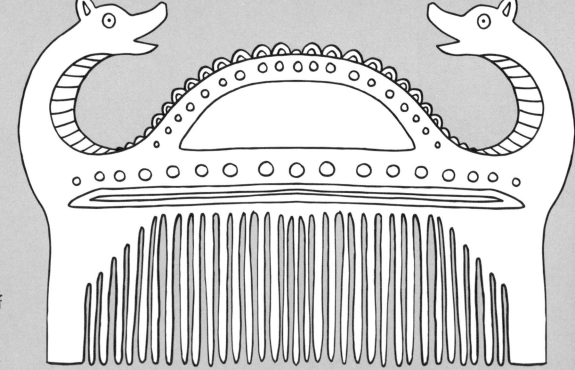

As well as being letters, runes can represent whole words. Using the key below, put rune stickers in the right places in this story.

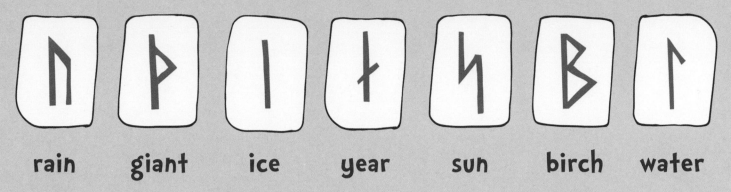

rain   giant   ice   year   sun   birch   water

Ulf was very proud of his hair and beard. He kept them tidy with his favorite comb. It was made of ☐ and beautifully decorated. But one day he couldn't find it anywhere. He went out in the ☐ hunting for his comb and got soaked through. Then he went out in the ☐ and got very hot, but still he could not find it.

For a whole ☐ he looked for his comb and all the while his beard and hair grew more messy. Then one winter's day Ulf's friend Astrid was standing by the frozen lake, gazing at the ☐. Gradually it melted and when she looked into the ☐ she spotted something with some runes written on it. She could not reach it, but luckily a friendly ☐ was passing and he fished it out. Then she saw that it was a comb—with the name "Ulf" written on it!

When Ulf was reunited with his beloved comb he was very happy indeed. He held a party in Astrid's honor—and made sure his hair and beard were neatly combed for the occasion.

Shield differences

Which of these two shields are the odd ones out? Work that out, then color them all in.

Recycled letters

Complete the words below using the letters from the word VIKING.

OD_N

_ISOR

_NIFE

RU_E

LON_SHIP

F_GUREHEAD

Long way home

Vikings lived in rectangular buildings known as longhouses. Can you help this farmer find his way home without getting caught by wolves?

Silly Vikings

What did the Viking say when he bought a lottery ticket?

"This could be my Loki day."

Why didn't the Viking write on the table?

She didn't want to rune it.

Why didn't the Norseman buy a new longship?

He couldn't afjord it.

Home on the farm

When the Vikings settled in a new place they would set up farms to produce food. Everyone in the family, including the children, would work on the land and look after the animals. On a Norse farm they would grow vegetables such as carrots, parsnips, cabbages, and onions, and grains such as barley, rye, and oats. There would be cattle, sheep, pigs, goats, horses, and chickens. Use the stickers to add life to this scene.

Food for thought

Gorm the Greedy is preparing for a family feast, but he couldn't resist having a snack as he laid things out on the table. Can you check against the list to see what items Gorm has already eaten?

Dried fish
Rye bread
Eggs
Turnips
Cheese
Butter
Peas
Carrots
Chicken

Norse horses

Vikings used horses to travel over land and to move heavy loads. Do the math problems to work out which is the strongest of these horses. The highest number is the strongest.

3 + 9 – 5 =

8 – 6 + 10 =

4 + 7 – 1 =

Make a Viking shield

Viking shields had lots of different patterns on them. You can copy our design or experiment with your own.

Ask a grown-up to help!

You'll need:

piece of sturdy cardboard

pencil

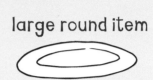
large round item

scissors

ruler

egg carton

glue

acrylic paint in two colors and paintbrush

silver duct tape

1. Take your piece of cardboard (an old box is ideal) and draw a large circle on it by using a tea tray or a large plate as a template. Cut it out with scissors.

2. Divide the circle into four sections by drawing two lines through the middle to make a cross.

3. Paint two opposite sections in one color and the other two sections in another. Leave to dry.

4. Cut out one of the cup shapes from the egg carton. Cover it in duct tape.

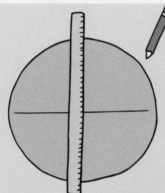

5. Put strips of duct tape across the shield to divide the four sections.

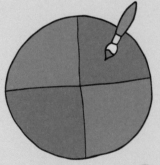

6. Stick duct tape around the edge of the shield. It will be easier to do this by overlapping lots of small bits of tape.

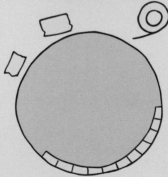

7. Stick the piece of egg carton in the center of the shield.

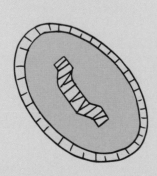

8. Cut out a strip from the leftover cardboard, cover it with duct tape, and attach it to the back of the shield with more tape to make a handle.

9. Now you're all set to defend yourself like a Viking!

New faces

These longships have lost their figureheads. Draw new scary faces on the front of these ships.

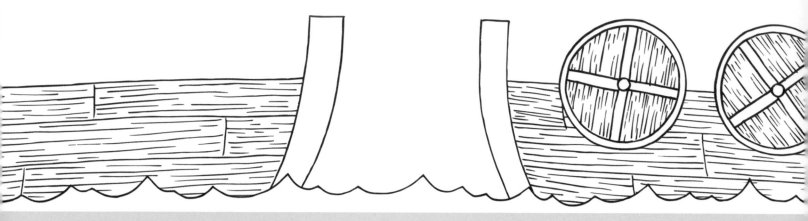

Helmet connections

Match these warriors to their helmets and draw a line between them. There is one odd helmet out. Which one is it?

Another thing

To make decisions and sort out arguments, Norse people would have a meeting called a Thing. These Vikings have been arguing about who owns a bit of land, and the judge, known as the law speaker, has awarded it to the person who has red hair, an oval brooch, and a green cloak. Which one is it?

Roving ravens

Odin's ravens, Huginn and Muninn, have been off on a fact-finding mission. Help them get back to Odin to pass on the information they've gathered.

What's your Viking name?

To work out the first part of your Viking name, count how many letters there are in your first name. Pick one of the names corresponding to that number in the list below. If there are 10 or more letters, add the digits together to get a number between 1 and 9.

So if your name is Constantine, that has 11 letters. Add 1 + 1 to get 2. Your Viking first name is Bjorn or Frida.

To work out the second part of your Viking name, pick the option that corresponds with the month you were born in.

First name

1   Olaf or Astrid
2   Bjorn or Frida
3   Erik or Hilda
4   Harald or Helga
5   Magnus or Inga
6   Leif or Tove
7   Torsten or Gudrun
8   Ulf or Gertrud
9   Snorri or Thora

Second name

January	the Red
February	the Dauntless
March	Flatnose
April	Barelegs
May	Sound Filler
June	the Wise
July	the Law Maker
August	the Adventurer
September	the Fleet Footed
October	Troll Hunter
November	Word Master
December	Slender Leg

Now work out the Viking names for all your friends and family!

28

Odd keys out

Vikings used decorated keys to lock chests containing their precious things.
Can you spot the two odd keys out?

Creature counting

This Viking fleet is arriving in Newfoundland, which is now in Canada. Lots of creatures are there to greet them. How many of each can you see?

Seals

Whales

Narwhals

Dolphins

Puffins

29

Home comforts

Many Viking families lived together in one big room in a longhouse. It would have been very dark, crowded, noisy, and smelly inside! Read about the different parts of their homes, then place the right sticker in the spaces.

Fireplace
This was the heart of the home, used for heat, light, and cooking.

Beds
Around the walls were raised areas that were used for sleeping and sitting on.

Walls
The walls were made of wood and sealed with mud to keep out drafts. There were no windows so it was quite dark inside.

Roof
The roof was made of turf or thatch, with a hole for the fire smoke to get out.

Lamps
Stone lamps full of fish oil were used to provide light inside the house.

Loom
The Vikings would weave cloth on looms leant against the walls. They would use wool from their sheep to make clothing.

Animals
The family's animals would often live at one end of the house.

Legend wordsearch

Can you find the characters from Norse stories hidden in this puzzle?

BALDR
BRAGI
FRIGG
HUGINN
LOKI
MUNINN
ODIN
SIGURD
SLEIPNIR
THOR

```
G H X C B R Y H K P S L H Q P Y H B V
L F B M S S I G U R D V N V L Z U T D
N R P G D L W T R S N D S B M L G L S
X I R T R E F H S W F H T L O K I D M
N G N V B I K R T G K P S R A G N T S
C G Z X J P S N K U D Z I G P N N K M
Q F S Z M N Y K D H T S G I N Q C B U
R T X R A I Q L Z Y H P M N K W N S N
O P G Q H R P S Q V O K H J L A D P I
D R M G R S B A L D R X W C S Z R K N
I S N B G X R D J L A R B R A G I Q N
N R W G R M S P W N Z S R M G Z B S Z
```

Smoke screen

Viking houses were very dark and smoky inside so these animals have almost disappeared. Draw in the rest of their outlines, then color them in.

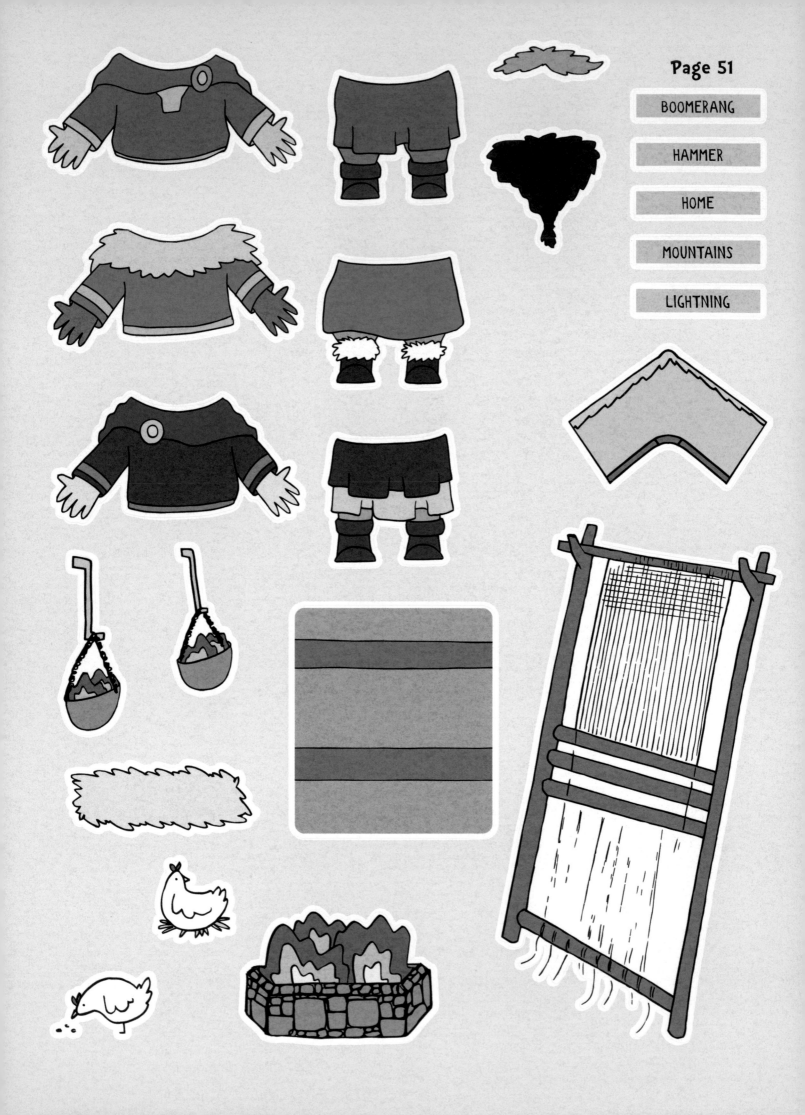

BOOMERANG

HAMMER

HOME

MOUNTAINS

LIGHTNING

Pages 4-5

Iceland

Greenland

Newfoundland

British Isles

Page 41

NORSE

ADVENTURES

THUNDER

BRIDGE

HUMANS

ODIN

SAGAS

LOKI

CASTLES

Page 19

Silver

Leather

Wheat

Spices

Silk

Wool

Downhill all the way

Vikings were good skiers and in fact the word "ski" comes from the Old Norse word for snowshoe. Can you work out which of these skiers will get down the mountain to the village safely, without getting lost in the woods?

Mitts and match

Woven gloves and mittens were worn by the Norse people in cold weather. These have gotten mixed up! Draw lines to match them up, then color them in.

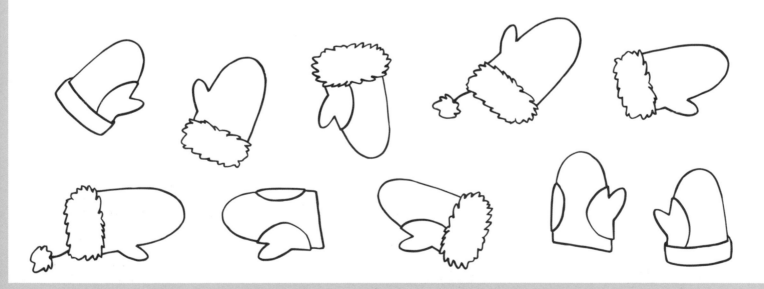

Make a longship lunch

To serve 2 people, you'll need:

banana

carrot

raisins

knife

jelly

Ask a grown-up to help!

2 small slices of bread

2 breadsticks

blueberries

1. Remove the peel from the banana and cut it in half lengthwise.

2. Cut about 2 inches off one end of each banana piece.

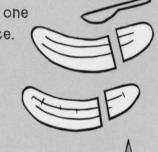

3. Place each banana on a plate. Position the cut-off end with the curved side down.

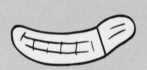

4. Slice your clean carrot into 8 rounds. Cut some small pieces to use as ears and a tongue for your figurehead.

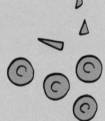

5. Cut away some of the banana to shape the figurehead and the tail. Add a scary face to the front of your longship using a raisin for the eye and the bits of carrot for ears and a tongue.

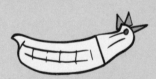

6. Place 4 carrot rounds along the side of each banana as shields. Put raisins in the center of each one.

7. Place a breadstick above the middle of each banana as a mast.

8. Add a piece of bread on top as a sail. Dot rows of jelly and spread them carefully to make stripes.

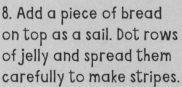

9. Make some sea under your longships with blueberries, then dig in!

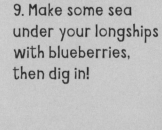

Dotty longhouse

Join the dots to complete this Viking home.

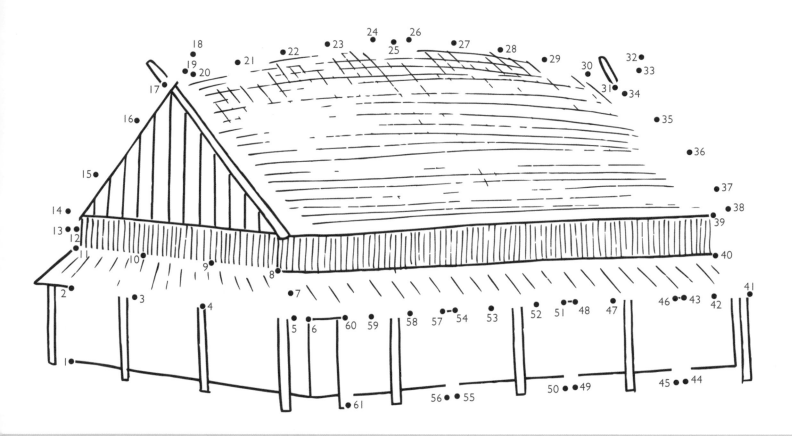

Funny Vikings

Why didn't the Viking want to talk about the god of thunder?

It was a Thor subject.

What is a Viking's favorite sweet treat?

Maca-runes.

How did Vikings send secret messages?

By using Norse code.

35

Plain sailing

Longships were designed for raids. Number the special features of this longship to match the descriptions below, then color in the picture.

1 The ships were built of overlapping planks of wood, which made them light and strong. This meant they could sail long distances. The sailors could also pick the ship up and carry it over land.

2 The carved figureheads at the front of the ships were designed to scare people when the Vikings arrived on a raid.

3 The ships could have as many as 50 oars, so they could go very fast. The people would take turns at rowing and resting so they could go faster for longer.

4 Sails made of wool or linen meant that the Vikings could use the wind to move the ship. The sails were made of strips of cloth sewn together to make stripes.

5 The ships were shallow so the Vikings could sail up rivers and land on beaches.

6 While they were at sea the Vikings stored their shields on the side of the ship to give extra protection from the waves.

7 Longships were pointed at both ends so they could go backwards without turning the boat around. Handy for a speedy getaway!

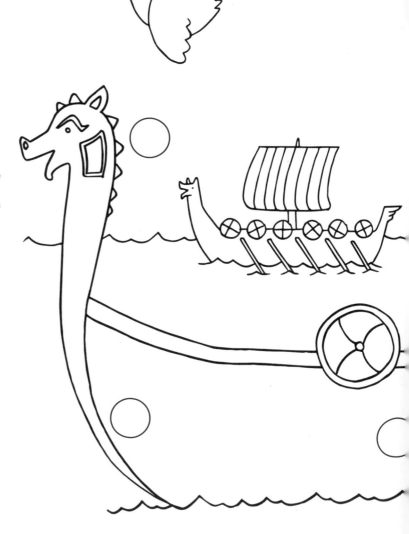

Colorful character

Harald Bluetooth was a Danish king who got his nickname from a noticeable bad tooth. He was also known for bringing different tribes together, which is why Bluetooth technology took his name. You can see that the rune initials on Harald's helmet are very similar to the modern Bluetooth logo.

Color in this picture of him, not forgetting his blue tooth!

Ready for battle

These warriors are off on a raid but need to get equipped first. Add some helmets, shields, and swords from the sticker pages.

Make a Viking beard

You'll need:

tape measure

Piece of fake fur about 12 inches square

 scissors

 12 inches of elastic

marker pen

 Ask a grown-up to help!

1. Measure your face from ear to ear and from your nose to where you want your beard to stop.

2. Mark this size on the back of your piece of fur with marker pen.

3. Now draw the shape you want your beard to be within this. Make the bottom and top of the beard curved.

4. Cut your piece of fabric out, parting the fur where you are cutting so you don't cut the fluffiness off.

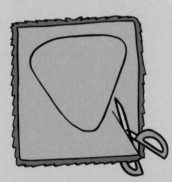

5. In the center, about half an inch from the top, cut out a semicircle for your mouth.

6. At either side at the top cut two small holes, about half an inch in from the edge.

7. Thread the elastic through one hole and tie a secure knot.

8. Holding your beard in position on your face, pass the elastic round the back of your head and through the other hole. Pull the elastic tight enough to hold the beard on and tie another knot.

9. Fluff the fur to hide the knots and wear your beard with pride!

39

Food wordsearch

Can you spot these Norse foods hiding in the grid?

PORRIDGE
HERRING
EGGS
MUSSELS
CABBAGE
TURNIP
ONION
LEEK
BARLEY
WHALE

```
O N I O N X T P Q M L M B
X Z F S D C A B B A G E X
S E N V K H S L P N V L G
Y G T W R N L Z W Z G K P
D G M X J S E I Q F D J R
X S T F B H E R R I N G L
B N U P R Q K E T C Q L M
M K R T V G D R I D G N U
W F N G N B L X M N H P S
H Q I S C A Z N Y W G F S
A W P O R R I D G E X K E
L X J C Q L M B C J K D L
E H D S I E N C N J F J S
K L M D G Y H X G S N S Z
```

Fiery funeral

The sea was so important to the Norse people that when they died some were buried in a ship along with their favorite things. Others were launched out to sea in a ship that was set on fire. Color in this flaming longship.

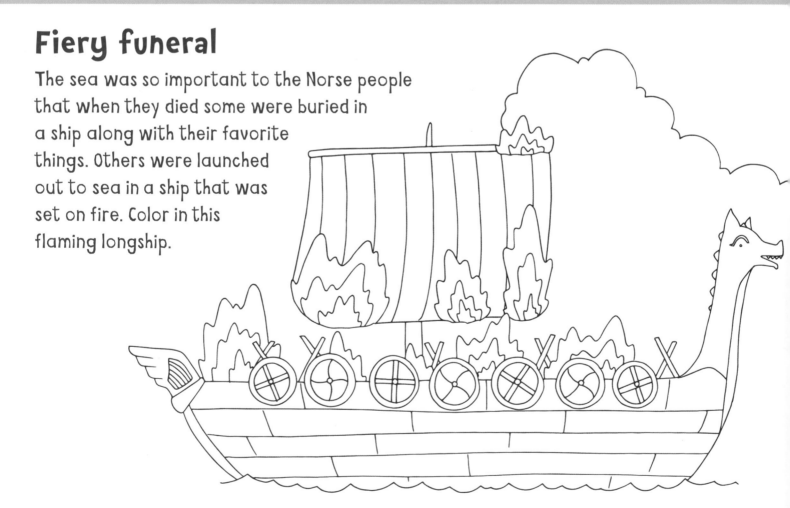

Tall tales

Learn more about Viking sagas by using the stickers to replace the jumbled words. Color in the picture and draw a rainbow bridge between Asgard and Midgard.

In the evenings, the Vikings loved to tell stories known as [GASAS]. These tales were about [TADURVENES], feuds, and the [SNERO] gods. Characters included [DONI], the father of the gods, [KILO], the shapeshifting god of fire, and Thor, the god of [DERHUNT]. The gods all lived in shining [STALCES] in a beautiful kingdom called Asgard. This kingdom is connected to Midgard, where [MUNSAH] live, by a rainbow [GIRDEB] called Bifrost.

Asgard

Midgard

41

The Vikings are coming!

A fleet of longships is arriving on a raid. Add stickers to show the arrival of the warriors and the local people running away.

Rune cakes

Make some delicious cakes and decorate them with Viking runes.

Ask a grown-up to help!

You'll need:

 2 eggs

 1 muffin tray

 1 stick of butter, softened

 half a cup self-rising flour

 12 cupcake liners

 half a cup superfine sugar

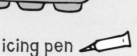 1 cup powdered sugar

water

icing pen

1. Set your oven to 350°F. Place 12 paper cupcake liners in a muffin tray.

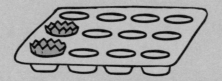

2. Beat the softened butter and superfine sugar together until light and fluffy.

3. Mix in 2 beaten eggs, a little at a time.

4. Sieve the self-rising flour and carefully fold it in.

5. Spoon the mixture into the cupcake liners. Bake in the oven for 15 to 20 minutes. Allow to cool while you make the icing.

6. Heat some water until it is warm, but not hot.

7. Sift the powdered sugar into a bowl and add a tablespoon of warm water. Mix until smooth and thick enough to coat the back of a spoon. Add more water if necessary.

8. When the cakes are cool, pour enough icing on each one to cover the top.

9. Once the icing has set, draw runes on the cakes with the icing pen.

ᛦ ᚴ ᛮ ᛒ ᛏ ᛅ ᛲ ᚼ
ᚦ ᛏ ᛯ ᛉ ᛘ ᛃ ᛩ ᛁ

Mixing drinks

Norse people drank out of animal horns and also out of glass, wooden, and metal cups. These Vikings have gotten their drinks mixed up. Follow the tangled lines to match them up.

Not to be mist

This longship has gotten lost in the sea mist. Draw over the outline so it can find its way home. Then color the picture in.

Cargo counting

Knarrs were wider, slower boats than longships. They were used to move goods and livestock. Can you count how many of the following are being carried on this knarr?

- Bales of wool
- Sheaves of wheat
- Sheep
- Cattle
- Chickens

Party time

In Norse mythology, Valhalla is an enormous banquet hall where warriors chosen by the god Odin are taken if they die in battle. Color in this picture of the feasting and fun.

Wolf double

Geri and Freki were Odin's two wolf companions. Draw Freki by copying this drawing of Geri. Use the grid to help you.

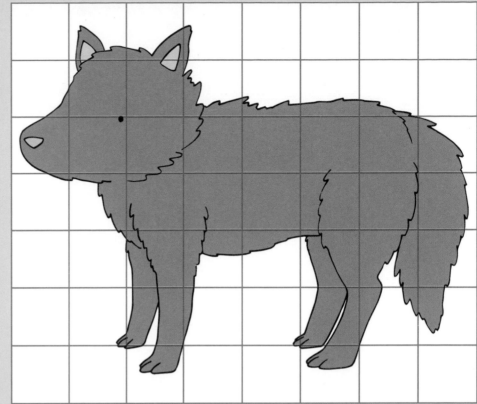

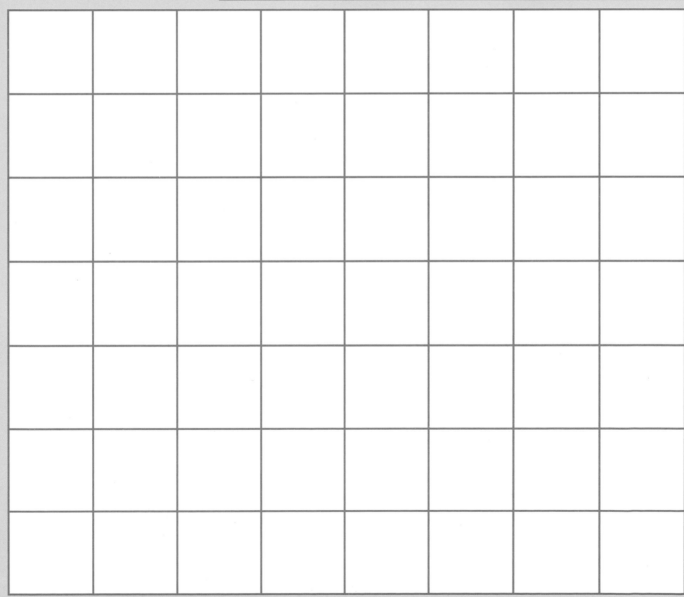

Odd Valkyrie out

Viking warriors hoped that if they died in battle, beautiful Valkyries would come to carry them to Valhalla for a party. Can you spot which of these Valkyries is the odd one out?

Dotty farm animal

Join the dots to find out what kind of Norse farm animal this is.

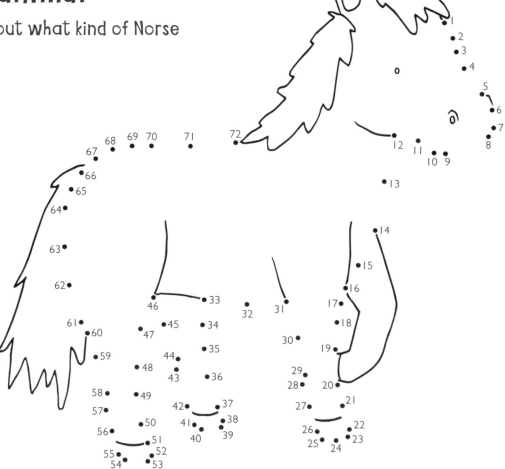

Winter preparations

Because the winters were long and cold, the Norse people had to do lots to get ready for them. Can you work out what's happening in these pictures and number them?

1 Gathering firewood

2 Drying fish

3 Smoking meat

4 Rounding up the animals

5 Harvesting hay to feed the animals

6 Pickling vegetables

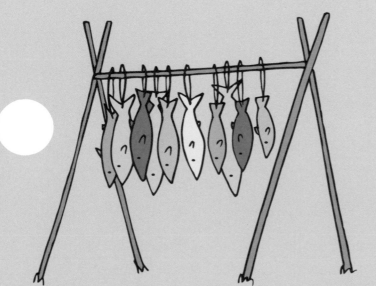

Savage checkmates

Even Viking warriors loved playing board games, which were scratched onto wood, stone, or leather. Some Norse chess pieces were discovered in 1831 and called the Lewis chessmen after the Scottish island they were found on. Find the matching pairs and circle the odd chess piece out.

Tangled tunes

Vikings loved music and would hold feasts with dancing and singing. Follow the lines to match these musicians to their instruments.

Flute

Pan pipes

Mouth harp

Thor inspiring

Use the stickers to replace the jumbled words in this story. Then color in the picture of Thor in his chariot.

Thor, the god of thunder, was in charge of guarding Asgard, the | MOEH |

of the gods. To do this he used a special hammer, so strong it could crush

| STAINOMUN | . Vikings believed that the noise of thunder was Thor using his

hammer to fight his foes. If he threw this hammer at an enemy it would come straight

back to his hands again, like a | ERBANGOOM | . Thor's magic hammer was called

Mjöllnir, and the Vikings thought that | NILGNIGHT | was caused by sparks flying

off the hammer when it hit things. Thor rode across the sky in a chariot pulled by

goats, which he would sometimes kill and eat. Then he would bless them with his

| MERMAH | to bring them back to life again!

Up Helly Aa!

In Shetland, in the very north of Scotland, they celebrate their Viking heritage with fire festivals called Up Helly Aa. Add stickers to bring this fiery procession to life.

Leif's travels

Leif Erikson was a Viking explorer who discovered a place that he called Vinland because of the grapevines growing there. Help Leif through the sea maze to get to the green lands of Vinland, avoiding icy Greenland.

Beach raid

When Vikings arrived on a raid, they could sail their shallow boats right up onto the beach and surprise the locals. Can you spot five differences between these pictures?

Make a fiery torch

If you fancy having a Viking procession, you'll need a fiery torch.

You'll need:

 Piece of dark-colored paper, about 12 x 8 inches

 Sticky tape

 Scissors

 Tissue paper in yellow, orange, and red

1. Roll up your piece of paper so that it forms a cone shape.

2. Use sticky tape to hold it in position.

3. Cut three rectangles of tissue paper about 10 x 6 inches in red, orange, and yellow.

4. Along the long edge, cut triangles out to make a jagged edge.

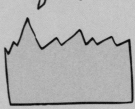

5. Place the orange tissue paper on the red paper and the yellow on top of that, with the long straight edges lined up.

6. Scrunch the straight edges together to make your flame.

7. Stick it into the top of your cone to make your torch.

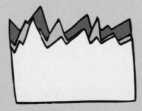

8. Now you're ready for a Viking procession!

Misplaced letters

Unscramble these letters to make a list of places that the Vikings raided or settled in.

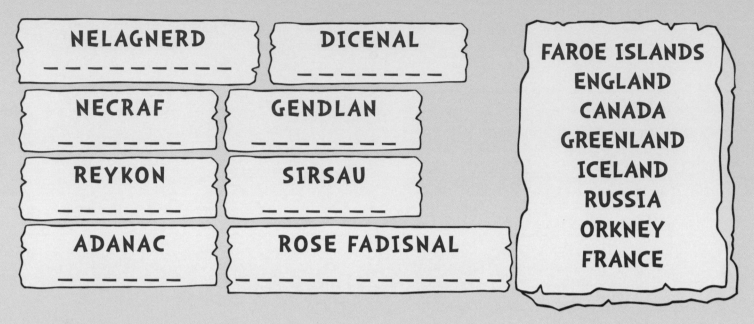

NELAGNERD	DICENAL
_ _ _ _ _ _ _ _ _	_ _ _ _ _ _ _

NECRAF	GENDLAN
_ _ _ _ _ _	_ _ _ _ _ _ _

REYKON	SIRSAU
_ _ _ _ _ _	_ _ _ _ _ _

ADANAC	ROSE FADISNAL
_ _ _ _ _ _	_ _ _ _ _ _ _ _ _ _ _

FAROE ISLANDS
ENGLAND
CANADA
GREENLAND
ICELAND
RUSSIA
ORKNEY
FRANCE

Stolen treasure

Which of these fearsome warriors is going to return from the raid with the biggest haul?
Do the math problems to see who got the most.

7 + 5 − 1 =

3 + 6 + 5 =

1 + 9 + 8 =

Which weapon?

Vikings were famed for their weapons. This warrior is deciding what to take into battle with her. The item she's decided on is sharp, has a carved handle, and is half as tall as she is. Can you work out which one it is?

Ship shape

Viking longships were very fast as they were powered by both sail and oars. Can you work out which of these ships matches the silhouette?

The world of the Vikings (pages 4-5)

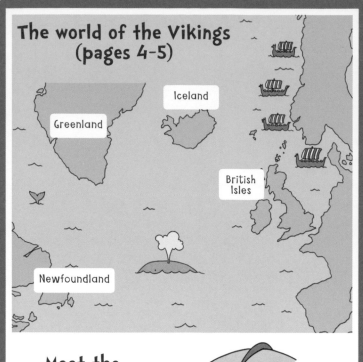

Greenland
Iceland
British Isles
Newfoundland

Tall order (page 7)

2 1 5 3 4

Get packing (page 8)

Missing oar and drinking horn

Meet the Viking warrior (page 6)

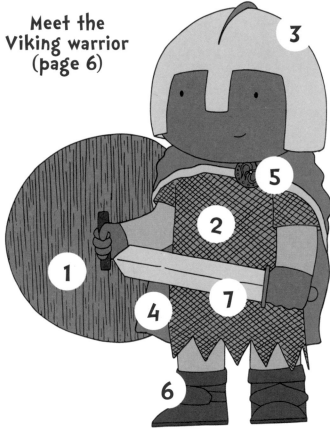

Norse jobs (page 9)

basketmaker
farmer
boatbuilder
jeweler

Odd figurehead out (page 7)

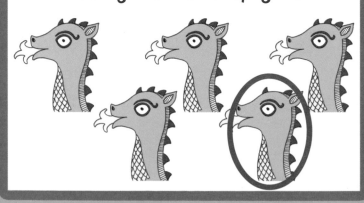

Raven guide (page 9)

Norse myths (pages 10-11)

Odin

Baldr

Bragi

Loki

Frigg

Thor

Odd brooch out (page 12)

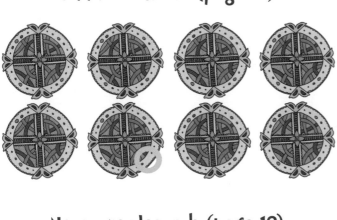

Norse wordsearch (page 12)

Longship races (page 13)

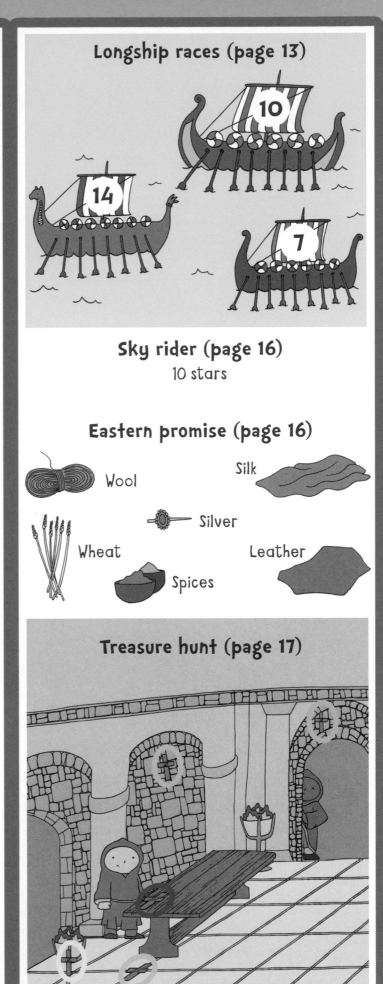

Sky rider (page 16)
10 stars

Eastern promise (page 16)

Wool

Silk

Wheat

Silver

Spices

Leather

Treasure hunt (page 17)

Norse code (page 19)

Ulf was very proud of his hair and beard. He kept them tidy with his favorite comb. It was made of [ᛒ] and beautifully decorated. But one day he couldn't find it anywhere. He went out in the [ᚾ] hunting for his comb and got soaked through. Then he went out in the [ᛋ] and got very hot, but still he could not find it.

For a whole [ᛉ] he looked for his comb and all the while his beard and hair grew more messy. Then one winter's day Ulf's friend Astrid was standing by the frozen lake, gazing at the [ᛁ]. Gradually it melted and when she looked into the [ᚨ] she spotted something with some runes written on it. She could not reach it but luckily a friendly [ᚦ] was passing and he fished it out. Then she saw that it was a comb—with the name "Ulf" written on it!

When Ulf was reunited with his beloved comb he was very happy indeed. He held a party in Astrid's honor—and made sure his hair and beard were neatly combed for the occasion.

Shield differences (page 20)

Recycled letters (page 20)

Odin

Visor

Knife

Rune

Longship

Figurehead

Long way home (page 21)

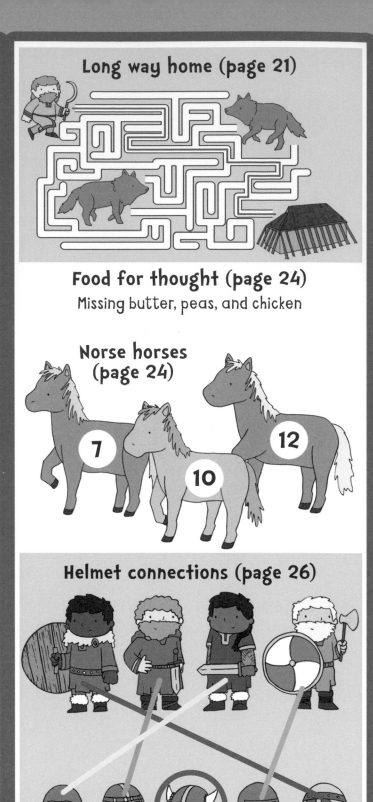

Food for thought (page 24)
Missing butter, peas, and chicken

Norse horses (page 24)

7   10   12

Helmet connections (page 26)

Another thing (page 27)

Roving ravens (page 27)

Odd keys out (page 29)

Creature counting (page 29)

Seals - 7 Narwhals - 2 Puffins - 4
Whales - 2 Dolphins - 3

Home comforts (pages 30-31)

Legend wordsearch (page 32)

```
G H X C B R Y H K P S L H Q P Y H B V
L F B M S S I G U R D V N V L Z U T D
N R P G D L W T R S N D S B M L G L D
X I R T R E F H S W F H T L O K I D M
N G N V B I K R T G K P S R A G I N T
C G Z X J P S N K U D Z I G P N K B S
Q F S Z M N Y K D H T S G I N Q C B U
R O R U T R A I G M S T H P U N W S N
O P G Q H R P S Q V O K H J L A D P I
D R M G R S B A L D R X W C S Z R K N
I S N B G X R D J L A R B R A G I Q N
N R W G R M S P W N Z S R M G Z B S Z
```

Downhill all the way (page 33)

Mitts and match (page 33)

Plain sailing (pages 36-37)

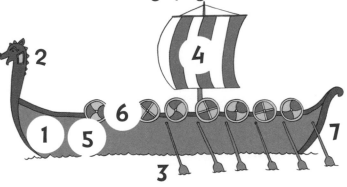

Food wordsearch (page 40)

```
O N I O N X T P Q M L M B
X Z F S D C A B B A G E X
S E N V K H S L P N V L G
Y G T W R N L Z W Z G K P
D G M X J S E I Q F D J R
X S T F B H E R R I N G L
B N U P R Q K E T C Q L M
M K U R N T V G D R I D N U
W F N G N B L X M N H P S
H Q I S C A Z N Y W G F S
A W P O R R I D G E X K E
L X J C Q L M B C J K D L
E H D S I E N C N J F J S
K L M D G Y H X G S N S Z
```

Tall tales (page 41)

In the evenings, the Vikings loved to tell stories known as SAGAS. These tales were about ADVENTURES, feuds and the NORSE gods. Characters included ODIN, the father of the gods, LOKI, the shapeshifting god of fire, and Thor the god of THUNDER. The gods all lived in shining CASTLES in a beautiful kingdom called Asgard. This kingdom is connected to Midgard where HUMANS live by a rainbow BRIDGE called Bifrost.

Mixing drinks (page 45)

Cargo counting (page 46)

Bales of wool – 2
Sheaves of wheat – 2
Sheep – 3
Cattle – 1
Chickens – 5

Odd Valkyrie out (page 48)

Winter preparations (page 49)

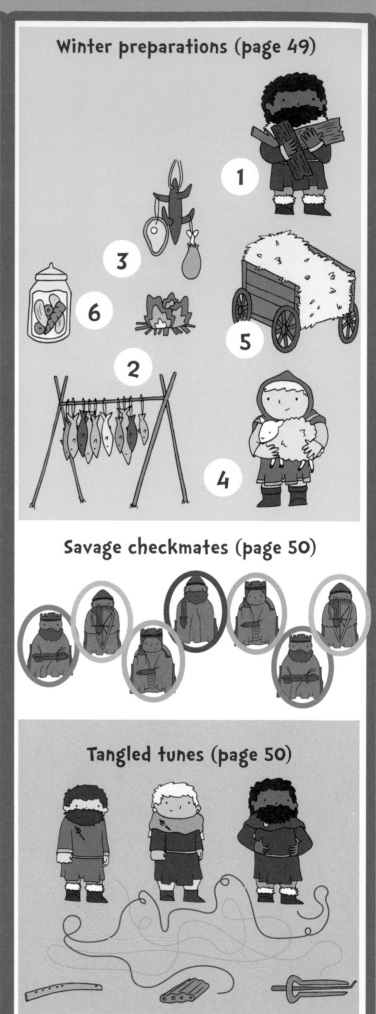

Savage checkmates (page 50)

Tangled tunes (page 50)

Thor inspiring (page 51)

Thor, the god of thunder, was in charge of guarding Asgard, the HOME of the gods. To do this he used a special hammer, so strong it could crush MOUNTAINS. Vikings believed that the noise of thunder was Thor using his hammer to fight his foes. If he threw this hammer at an enemy it would come straight back to his hands again, like a BOOMERANG. Thor's magic hammer was called Mjöllnir, and the Vikings thought that LIGHTNING was caused by sparks flying off the hammer when it hit things. Thor rode across the sky in a chariot pulled by goats, which he would sometimes kill and eat. Then he would bless them with his HAMMER to bring them back to life again!

Leif's travels (page 54)

Beach raid (page 54)

Misplaced letters (page 56)

Greenland | Iceland
France | England
Orkney | Russia
Canada | Faroe Islands

Stolen treasure (page 56)

11   **14**   **18**

Which weapon? (page 57)

Ship shape (page 57)

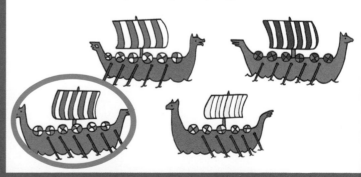

First published 2020 by Button Books, an imprint of Guild of Master Craftsman Publications Ltd, Castle Place, 166 High Street, Lewes, East Sussex, BN7 1XU, UK. Text © GMC Publications Ltd, 2020. Copyright in the Work © GMC Publications Ltd, 2020. Illustrations © 2020 Jennifer Alliston. ISBN 978 1 78708 075 1. Distributed by Publishers Group West in the United States. All rights reserved. The right of Jennifer Alliston to be identified as the illustrator of this work has been asserted in accordance with the Copyright, Designs, and Patents Act 1988, sections 77 and 78. No part of this publication may be reproduced, stored in a retrieval system, or transmitted in any form or by any means without the prior permission of the publisher and copyright owner. While every effort has been made to obtain permission from the copyright holders for all material used in this book, the publishers will be pleased to hear from anyone who has not been appropriately acknowledged and to make the correction in future reprints. The publishers and author can accept no legal responsibility for any consequences arising from the application of information, advice, or instructions given in this publication. A catalog record for this book is available from the British Library. Publisher: Jonathan Bailey. Production: Jim Bulley and Jo Pallett. Senior Project Editor/Text: Wendy McAngus. Managing Art Editor: Gilda Pacitti. Color origination by GMC Reprographics. Printed and bound in China. Warning! Choking hazard—small parts. Not suitable for children under 3 years.